GW01045178

the foursome

the foursome

E. A. WHITEHEAD

FABER AND FABER
3 Queen Square
London

First published in 1972
by Faber and Faber Limited
3 Queen Square London WC1
Printed in Great Britain by
Latimer Trend & Co Ltd Plymouth
All rights reserved

ISBN 0 571 09879 7 (*paper covered edition*)
ISBN 0 571 09878 9 (*hard covered edition*)

All enquiries regarding amateur or professional production of this play should be addressed in the first instance to Margaret Ramsay Ltd., 14a Goodwin's Court, St. Martin's Lane, London W.C.2.

for Mike Simpson

Characters

HARRY   Early twenties
TIM   Late twenties
MARIE   About twenty
BELLA   Nineteen

The action takes place in a hollow in the
sandhills at Freshfield, near Liverpool

THE FOURSOME was first performed at The Theatre Upstairs at the Royal Court Theatre on 17th March 1971. The cast was as follows:

Harry	PAUL ANGELIS
Tim	PHILIP DONAGHY
Marie	CLARE SUTCLIFFE
Bella	SHARON DUCE

Directed by JONATHAN HALES
Designed by JOHN NAPIER
Lighting by LIZ WELLS

This production was presented by Michael Codron, by arrangement with the Royal Court Theatre, at the Fortune Theatre on 4th May 1971. The part of Tim was played by James Hazeldine.

act one

Scene: Before the lights come up, the sound of birds is heard. Then the sound of pop music, slowly getting louder as the LIGHTS COME UP SLOWLY. *The lights reach glaring intensity on a scene of baked white sand and blue sky as the music becomes deafening.*

HARRY *appears at the top of the dune and stands surveying the hollow. He carries a beach bag and a transistor radio.* TIM *joins him. He carries a beach bag and a wad of newspapers. Both men wear sweatshirts and jeans.*

HARRY *looks behind across the sand.* TIM *does the same. They grin at each other.* HARRY *snaps off the transistor. For a second they stand poised looking at the hollow in silence.*

HARRY: OK?
TIM (*hesitant. Looking all round the scene*): Hunh.
HARRY: What?
TIM: You wanna go on a bit?
HARRY: I'm fucked.
TIM: We go further than this.
HARRY: No need.
TIM: We better hang on for them.
HARRY: What are they doing?
TIM (*looking*): They're coming up.
HARRY: I can't see them.
TIM (*points*): They're coming round there.
> (HARRY *jumps down into the hollow. Sprawls on his back. Stares at the sky, stretches his arms.*)
HARRY (*luxuriating*): Ahhhhhhhhhhhhh.
TIM: They're sitting down there.

HARRY: Give them a shout.
  (TIM *waves*.)
HARRY (*shouts*): Now arse!
TIM: They'll hear you.
HARRY (*shouts*): NOW ARSE!
TIM: They heard you.
HARRY: They'd hear me whisper. (*Whispers*) Now arse . . .
TIM: They're not moving.
HARRY: They're playing hard to get.
  (HARRY *empties his bag and begins to spread a towel*.)
  Come on . . . give us a hand . . .
TIM: Now they'll stay down there.
HARRY: You bet?
  (TIM *comes down and helps* HARRY *to lay out the things*.)
  They're gasping for it.
TIM: Yours is.
HARRY: So is yours.
TIM (*grins; prissy*): So am I . . .
HARRY (*grins; prissy*): So am I, dear . . .
TIM: Everybody's gasping for it . . .
  (HARRY *stretches*)
HARRY (*ecstatic*): Godddddddd.
  (*Both men sprawl on their towels, left stage*.)
TIM: It's gonna be a scorcher.
HARRY: No . . . serious like . . . I think you're on there, mate.
TIM (*unsure*): Hunh.
HARRY: I think you're definitely on . . . don't you?
TIM: I'll tear the arse off it.
HARRY (*laughs; prissy*): Save some for me, sweetheart . . .
TIM (*prissy*): For you I'll draw on me reserves . . .
HARRY (*laughing*): Second shot's best.
TIM: You know what she said last night?
HARRY (*giggly*): Go on . . .
TIM: She said I looked like a . . . when we were lying in the back
  of the van . . .
HARRY (*coy*): I remember . . .
TIM: She said I looked like a Spaniard.
HARRY (*wide-eyed*): A bullfighter!

TIM: No, a Spaniard.

HARRY (*prissy*): She meant a bullfighter. That's all these cows think about . . . bullfighters.

TIM (*mock-vain*): Mind you . . . I think there is a bit of the Spaniard in me.

HARRY: I think there was a bit of the Spaniard in her too.

TIM (*mock-angry*): Oh yeah . . . I saw you piping . . . in the mirror.

HARRY: All I could see was a big white arse.

TIM (*prissy*): Well it wasn't mine.

HARRY (*prissy*): I *knew* it wasn't yours, of course.

TIM: Huh!

HARRY: Anyway . . . you can talk . . . I drove fourteen times round the Pier Head while you were at it.

TIM: You got stuck on the roundabout.

HARRY: Who got stuck on the roundabout?

(*Both men laugh. Pause.*)

It's gonna be a great day.

TIM: Did *you* get it away?

HARRY: What?

TIM: Last night . . . did you get your end away?

HARRY (*mock-shock*): I'd only just met her.

TIM: Did that worry you?

HARRY: No . . . it worried her.

TIM (*ironic*): She looked a bit shy . . .

HARRY: I think she had the rags up.

TIM (*prissy*): And how would you know?

HARRY: I had a bit of finger pie.

TIM (*laughing*): Did you lick your fingers after?

(HARRY *laughs and lies loudly sniffing his fingers.*)

(*Laughing.*) The van smelt like a fish shop after.

HARRY (*wry*): It smells like a bloody scent counter this morning.

TIM (*wry*): Yeah . . . they . . .

(*Pause.*)

HARRY: Pass us an orange.

(TIM *takes an orange from the bag and throws it to* HARRY— *wide.* HARRY *catches it.*)

(*Generous.*) Have one yourself.

13

TIM: Gee thanks, kid.

(TIM *takes an orange. They eat.*)

HARRY: Where are they?

TIM: Waiting for us.

HARRY: They'll have to wait.

(*Pause.* TIM *collects the orange peel and puts it in a paper bag.*)

(*Mock-stern.*) And don't forget . . . we swop over at three o'clock.

TIM: Right, captain.

HARRY: Regardless.

TIM: Definitely. (*Pause.*) Hey . . .

HARRY: What?

TIM: Not if yours has got the rags up.

HARRY (*laughing*): Oh me darling!

(HARRY *grabs* TIM, *and both men fall back, wrestling and laughing.*)

(*Mock-Irish.*) Ye're all right dere . . . I'm telling you, lad . . . dere's no need to be worrying yerself . . . ye're all right dere . . . trust ould Danny . . .

TIM: Who's ould Danny when he's out?

HARRY: How would I know?

(*Both men lie back.* HARRY *fiddles with the transistor.*)

Where the fuck are they?

TIM: Go and get them.

HARRY (*prissy*): You go.

TIM: You picked them up . . .

HARRY (*arch*): They picked me up really.

(TIM *goes to the top of the dune and looks across.*)

(*Shouts.*) NOW ARSE!

TIM: Shut up.

HARRY: What?

TIM: They're coming up.

HARRY: Sit down.

(*Pause.* TIM *waves.*)

TIM: They look shagged.

HARRY: They must be psychic.

(TIM *stands waving.*)

14

Sit down.

TIM: They're waving.

HARRY: Come down.

(TIM *comes down.*)

TIM: I'm dying for a burst . . .

HARRY (*mocking*): Are you all excited?

TIM (*mock giggles*): Ohhh . . . I'll wet meself in a minute!

(TIM *goes off left to the woods.*)

(HARRY *lies back and closes his eyes.*)

(*After a minute the girls appear, close together. Both are very heavily made up, with hair lacquered and piled high. They wear tight sweaters and mini-skirts and heeled shoes. Each carries a tiny handbag.*)

(*They look at* HARRY.)

(HARRY *grins extravagantly and waves.*)

(*They clamber down daintily.*)

MARIE: Jesus . . . we shoulda brought a rope.

HARRY: Watch you don't twist anything.

(MARIE *staggers the last few steps and falls on* HARRY. *He grabs her.*)

(*Passionate.*) You're mine, mine, mine!

MARIE (*delighted*): Sod off!

(*The girls sit down, stage right.* MARIE *rubs her legs.* BELLA *lies back.*)

Me legs is killing me.

HARRY: Want me to rub them for you?

MARIE: I'm in enough trouble . . .

HARRY: Relax and strip off.

MARIE: It's far enough, isn't it?

HARRY (*coy*): If we go any farther we'll end up in the woods . . .

MARIE: I thought that was the idea?

HARRY: What? Yeah . . . to end up there . . . not to spend all day there . . .

MARIE (*giggling*): Hear that, Bella?

BELLA: What?

MARIE: We're gonna end up in the woods.

BELLA: Where's your mate?

HARRY: In the woods.

BELLA (*grinning*): What . . . already?

HARRY: He couldn't wait.

MARIE (*lying back*): Jesus . . . I'm beat.

HARRY: Relax . . . take your clothes off.

MARIE: He wants a free show.

HARRY (*coy*): I'll show you mine . . . if you'll show me yours.

MARIE: Me mam told me about boys like you.

HARRY: How did she know?

> (HARRY *rolls across and tries to kiss* MARIE. *She struggles, laughing.*)
>
> You're mine.

MARIE: Leggo! You're hurting me hand.

HARRY: Give us a kiss.

MARIE (*laughing*): Sod off!

HARRY: Resistance is useless.

MARIE: Help!

HARRY: Who can help you now?

TIM (*entering*): I!

HARRY: Curses! Returned!

> (TIM *leaps down and engages* HARRY *in a mock sword fight. He pushes* HARRY *down and transfixes him.*)

TIM: Die, dog!

HARRY (*sprawling*): Ahhhhhhhhh!

> (HARRY *dies then pushes* TIM *over.*)

TIM: You're dead.

HARRY: I recovered.

TIM (*mock-huffy*): If you won't be dead I'm not playing with you . . .

HARRY (*indulgent*): All right . . . all right then . . .

TIM: She's mine.

HARRY: All right . . .

MARIE: What?

TIM: You're mine.

MARIE: Am I?

> (TIM *tries to straddle her.* MARIE *throws him off.*)

TIM: You're mine now.

MARIE: Sod off!

TIM (*protesting*): I saved you from a fate worse than death.

MARIE: Thanks very much.

TIM: And that's all I get?

HARRY: Wasn't worth saving.

TIM: Wasting me time.

HARRY: Ungrateful bitch.

MARIE: Very nice!

TIM (*intense*): Seriously though . . .

HARRY: Eh?

TIM: Would you shaft her?

HARRY (*pointing to* MARIE): Her?

TIM: Yeah. Would you shaft her?

HARRY: You mean . . .

TIM: Would you?

HARRY (*reflective*): You mean if . . . if I loved her . . .

TIM: Of course.

HARRY: . . . and she loved me . . .

TIM: . . . and you were married . . .

HARRY: . . . and she was a Catholic . . .

    (*Pause.* HARRY *reflects.*)

TIM (*eager*): Would you?

HARRY (*snaps*): Right here on this blanket.

TIM (*mock-lecherous*): Here . . . in front of us?

HARRY (*shy*): Well . . . I mean . . . you wouldn't mind, would
    you? Would you?

TIM: Not if it was well done.

HARRY (*smug*): You know me . . .

TIM: I don't know her . . .

HARRY: That's true. (*Pause. He looks at* MARIE.) Are you good
    at it?

MARIE (*giggles*): Find out.

HARRY: Right.

    (HARRY *throws himself on* MARIE. *They wrestle. He pins her
    down.*)

MARIE: He's crazy.

HARRY: D'you fancy a bit?

MARIE: Sod off!

TIM: Don't excite him.

MARIE: He's exciting himself.

TIM (*asking a favour*): No . . . go easy with him. He's me only mate.

MARIE: Ow! Leggo!

TIM (*whispering*): Go easy . . .

MARIE: Tell him to let go.

TIM: He takes fits.

MARIE: Does he?

TIM: He foams at the thighs.

MARIE (*struggling*): I think he's taking one now.

(HARRY *suddenly releases her and lies back.*)

HARRY (*drawls*): Ahhh . . . God . . . that's better. I feel better for that.

MARIE (*laughing*): Are you all right now?

HARRY: That does a chap the world of good. Ahhh.

(HARRY *stretches and yawns luxuriously.*)

MARIE: Do you come here every weekend?

HARRY (*still the drawl*): Only if we pick anything up on Saturday night.

MARIE: Huh!

HARRY (*smug*): We're very selective . . .

MARIE (*dry*): Oh I'm made up.

HARRY: We don't just pick anyone up . . .

MARIE: Thanks.

HARRY: Pleasure.

MARIE: What's my name?

HARRY: Don't you know?

MARIE: I'm asking you.

HARRY: How would I know?

MARIE: I told you last night.

HARRY: There's no need to burst into tears.

MARIE (*laughing*): You don't remember.

HARRY: How could I forget?

MARIE: Do you?

HARRY: Of course I do.

MARIE: What is it then?

HARRY: Of course I remember. (*Pause.*) Albert.

MARIE: Cheeky sod!

HARRY: What's the matter?

MARIE: Last night you kept calling me Nelly.

HARRY: I was pissed.

MARIE (*sarcastic*): Were you . . . really?

(HARRY *lies back and closes his eyes.*)

HARRY: This is what I need.

(TIM *glances at a newspaper.* MARIE *looks in the beach bag.*)

MARIE: Got any butties?

TIM: What do you want?

MARIE: What are they?

TIM: There's cheese and tomato . . . or tomato and cheese.

(MARIE *takes a long drink from the bottle of lemonade.*)

Go easy . . . there's all day.

MARIE: I'm dead thirsty.

TIM: Have an orange.

MARIE: Ta.

(TIM *gives her an orange. She tosses the peel aside.*)

BELLA: Give us a slice.

MARIE: Have an orange.

BELLA: I only want a slice.

(MARIE *gives her a slice.*)

MARIE: I'm burning . . . Jesus . . .

HARRY: Take your stockings off.

MARIE: Aye aye.

HARRY: It's gonna get hotter.

MARIE: He's off again.

HARRY: You'll sweat like hell.

MARIE: I'm all right.

TIM (*to* BELLA): Why don't you?

BELLA: What?

TIM: Take your stockings off. Get your legs brown.

HARRY: You'll sweat to death if you don't.

BELLA: Are you, Marie?

MARIE (*to* HARRY): What about you?

HARRY: What?

MARIE: You'll sweat to death.

HARRY: You want me to strip?

MARIE (*giggling*): Do what you like. You're the one who's worried.

HARRY (*coy*): If I take my things off . . . will you take yours off?

MARIE: Sod off!

HARRY (*mock reluctance*): I see . . . OK. You want me to start. You want me to strip first.

MARIE: You suit yourself, lad.

HARRY: I'll do it . . . just to get some peace . . . I'll do it. I'll take my things off.

(HARRY *moves centre stage.* TIM *hums appropriate accompaniment.* HARRY *does his strip. His movements are slow, very stylised, mock-erotic. First he peels off his sweater and dances around the girls, teasing them with it.*)

MARIE (*giggling*). Look at that pot.

HARRY (*sticks out his stomach*): That is not a pot. That's muscle . . . in repose.

MARIE: You'll have a dirty big pot before long.

HARRY: And what about you, darling?

(HARRY *slips off his sandals, tosses one to* MARIE, *one to* BELLA. BELLA *ducks aside.* MARIE *picks up the sandal and slings it at* HARRY. *He ducks and it vanishes in the sand.* HARRY *looks briefly, resumes his strip.*)

(*Slowly he unbuckles his belt and dangles it suggestively before* MARIE. *She giggles and makes a grab for it.*)

Naughty! You'll be outa the club.

MARIE: You should be in the clubs.

(HARRY *lowers his jeans to his knees, waggles his pelvis. The girls look away, embarrassed, then look back, giggling.*)

(HARRY *drops his jeans, takes them off, repeats his dance.*)

(*He stands posing in string drawers, like Charles Atlas.*)

HARRY: Look at that. (*Showing his muscle.*) Just look at that. You too can have a body like mine.

MARIE: I'll stick to me own.

HARRY: You'll go blind.

MARIE: I bet he eats peanut butter.

HARRY: And now . . .

(HARRY *hooks his hands in his pants. Pause.*)

TIM (*shouting*): Get them down! Get them down!

HARRY (*to* TIM): With a roll on the drums and a blast on the trumpet . . .

(HARRY *slips off the string drawers and twirls them.* TIM

accompanies with music.)

MARIE (*laughing, looking away and back*): Dirty bugger!

HARRY: A beauty!

BELLA: Haven't you got a costume?

HARRY: I thought I'd give you a treat.

(*The girls giggle, look away, whisper to each other.* HARRY *puts on his trunks.*)

All right. Who's on next?

(HARRY *sits down and studies the girls.*)

MARIE: Him.

(MARIE *points to* TIM, *who turns away.*)

TIM: No.

HARRY: By popular demand . . .

BELLA: Aren't you getting changed?

TIM (*coy*): I'm not . . . hot . . .

BELLA: Go on.

MARIE: He's shy . . .

TIM (*prissy*): I am *not.*

BELLA: Are you shy?

TIM (*hiding his face*): Shucks . . . I . . . gee . . .

BELLA: Ahh . . . go on . . .

HARRY (*whisper*): His . . . torso . . . is divine . . .

(*Pause. Suddenly* TIM *turns front.*)

TIM (*elaborately bashful*): Ahh . . . now look . . . you're not . . . pulling my . . .

HARRY (*whisper*): I've never seen another like it.

MARIE: Go on!

BELLA: Yeah . . . go on . . .

TIM: Now . . . you . . . oh, all right then. But . . . but promise . . .

BELLA: What?

TIM (*writhing embarrassment*): You won't . . . you won't *look* at me . . . you won't look or anything?

BELLA: Look?

MARIE: We wouldn't *look* at you.

BELLA: Don't be soft.

TIM: I'd feel so . . . cheap.

MARIE: Go on then.

(TIM *fumbles and tugs at his sweater in a mock paroxysm of nervous modesty. He averts his head, giggles, looks coy, gasps, struggles with his buttons and manages to undo them with incredible slowness . . .*)

(MARIE *claps ironically.*)

(TIM *takes up one of the towels and holds it in front of himself with one hand while with the other he fumbles with his jeans and eventually slips out of them . . .*)

(MARIE *snatches away the towel.*)

(TIM *stands in black briefs and socks, hunching himself up and crossing his arms to hide his body.*)

(*Very appreciative.*) Aye aye aye aye.

BELLA: Sexy kecks.

TIM (*very coy*): They don't . . . take . . . much washing.

MARIE: I think they look great.

BELLA: You do look funny in your socks and drawers.

(TIM *whips off his briefs.*)

Dirty bugger!

MARIE: He's as bad as *he* is.

BELLA: They're both the same . . .

MARIE: Exhibitionists!

(*The girls laugh, glance away, glance back.*)

HARRY: A beauty.

MARIE: Dirty buggers!

(HARRY *claps.*)

(TIM *picks up the towel again and conceals himself with it as, clumsily, still standing, he takes off his socks and tosses one to* MARIE, *one to* BELLA. MARIE *throws it back.*)

(TIM *slips into his trunks and sits down.*)

You can get locked up for that.

TIM: Thousands do it every night.

HARRY (*pointing at* TIM'*s trunks*): Watch it, mate.

TIM: What?

HARRY: You're on show. (*Then to* MARIE.) Don't be piping, now.

MARIE: Who's piping?

TIM (*adjusting himself*): These bloody trunks were designed for a eunuch.

BELLA: A what?

22

TIM: A eunuch.

BELLA: What's a eunuch?

TIM: A man without a dick.

BELLA (*shocked*): Oh!

TIM (*reassuring*): Don't worry . . . I have. (*Pause.*) Are you coming into the woods now?

BELLA: No thanks.

MARIE: He's in a hurry.

TIM: Don't you want to?

BELLA (*laughs*): I wanna get some suntan.

HARRY: Take your clothes off.

MARIE: He's off again.

HARRY: You're sweating . . .

MARIE (*dry*): Must be the heat.

HARRY: Don't say I didn't warn you.

MARIE: I'm all right.

(HARRY *takes a bottle of suntan oil from the bag.*)

HARRY (*to* MARIE): Oil me.

MARIE: Oil yourself.

HARRY (*as if surprised*): Don't you want to oil me?

MARIE (*sarcastic*): Ohhh . . . I'd get carried away.

HARRY: That's all right as long as you don't spill the oil.

MARIE: OK.

HARRY: Put plenty on . . . but spread it.

MARIE: Yes, lover.

(MARIE *rubs the oil on* HARRY.)

HARRY: Christ!

MARIE (*jumps*): What?

HARRY: Your nails!

MARIE: Sorry . . . did I scratch you?

HARRY: You're tearing me to shreds.

(HARRY *examines her nails.*)

MARIE: I like them long. Don't you?

HARRY: You certainly do.

MARIE: Don't you?

HARRY: As long as they're not buried in me back.

MARIE: Lie down.

HARRY (*lying down*): Go easy with the talons,

23

MARIE (*rubbing*): Poor ickle babby . . .

HARRY (*twisting*): Ooohhhh.

MARIE: Is that nice?

HARRY: Lovely . . . aaahhh.

MARIE: You're lovely and firm . . .

HARRY: Do my legs.

(HARRY *lies back while* MARIE *rubs his legs.*)

MARIE: Ooohhh. . . . Aren't they smooth?

HARRY (*prissy*): They're covered in golden down.

MARIE (*stroking*): I think they're gorgeous . . .

HARRY (*smug, drawling*): Of course I look after myself.

MARIE: I bet you do.

HARRY: I'm the athletic type.

MARIE: Yeah?

HARRY: Can't get me off the rugger pitch, you know . . .

MARIE: No.

HARRY: Up all night with my chest expander . . .

MARIE: You look after your body . . .

HARRY: Oh I do indeed. If I look after anything, I look after my body. (*Pause.*) Well . . . it's the only one I have, you know.

MARIE: Turn over.

HARRY (*turns over*): Don't forget that.

MARIE: What?

HARRY (*points to his trunks*): That.

MARIE: You can oil that yourself.

HARRY: It's self-lubricating.

MARIE (*oiling his thighs*): Dirty bugger . . .

HARRY: Ahhhhh.

MARIE: I think he's gonna pass out . . .

HARRY: It's like a dream . . .

MARIE: Is it?

HARRY: . . . a wet dream . . .

(MARIE *puts the bottle down.*)

MARIE: You can oil yourself.

HARRY: Sorry . . . go on . . .

MARIE: You gonna behave?

HARRY (*childish*): Promise to be a good boy.

MARIE: All right.

24

HARRY: Do me back.

(HARRY *lies on his stomach while* MARIE *oils his back.*)

MARIE: You're nice and brown already.

HARRY: Don't forget my legs.

MARIE: I won't.

HARRY: Easy . . . that's sensitive.

MARIE: Sorry . . . is that all right?

HARRY: Lovely.

(MARIE *strokes the back of his legs, and his thighs.*)
Ahhhhh.

MARIE: All right?

HARRY (*twisting*): Ahhhh . . . aaaahhhhhh.

MARIE (*laughing*): I think he's in for a fit.

HARRY: AAAHHHHHHHH.

(HARRY *slumps.* MARIE *jumps.*)

MARIE: What's the matter?

HARRY (*groaning*): Ooohhh.

MARIE: Are you all right?

HARRY: Mmmmmm.

MARIE: What happened?

HARRY (*faint*): Eh?

MARIE (*grinning*): What happened then?

HARRY: I shot me load.

MARIE (*howls with laughter*): YOU WHAT?

HARRY (*weak*): I shot me load.

MARIE: What's that?

BELLA: He what?

HARRY: Ask your mam.

TIM: He was foaming at the thighs.

MARIE (*laughing*): Dirty bugger!

HARRY: I'll be all right in twenty-seven minutes.

MARIE: All right.

HARRY: I'll be ready by then.

MARIE (*grinning*): Ready for what?

HARRY: A bit of the other.

MARIE: You can sod off!

(HARRY *lies back, stretches luxuriously.*)

HARRY (*deep drawl*): God . . . what a super morning. I'm positive

it's going to be an absolutely super day. Isn't the sky
absolutely super? I think I'll have a little shut-eye . . . build
up my strength for later, darling.

(MARIE *lies near* BELLA.)

Keep your eye on him, Bella.

HARRY: Aren't you going to put any oil on yourself?

MARIE: I'm all right.

HARRY: You won't be for long. You'd better put some on or
you'll frizzle.

(MARIE *dabs some oil on her face and arms. Then she dabs her
stockings.*)

HARRY: Christ!

MARIE: What?

HARRY: Why don't you take them off?

MARIE: You go asleep.

HARRY: Nobody's gonna stare at you.

TIM: You speak for yourself.

(*Pause.* HARRY *sits up, stares at* MARIE.)

MARIE: What are you looking at?

HARRY: You could always go and get changed in the woods.

MARIE: Changed?

HARRY: You might just as well.

MARIE: Haven't got a costume.

(*Pause.*)

HARRY: I said we'd be coming to the beach.

MARIE: Huh.

HARRY: Why didn't you bring a costume?

MARIE (*emphatic*): I haven't *got* a costume.

HARRY: You haven't *got* a costume?

MARIE: I told you.

HARRY (*edgy*): Couldn't you borrow your grannie's or something?

MARIE: Me grannie hasn't got one either.

HARRY: Christ!

(*Pause.*)

(*To* BELLA) What about you?

BELLA: What?

HARRY: Have you?

(BELLA *shakes her head.*)

26

(HARRY *looks at* TIM, *then at the girls.*)

You're gonna melt away here when the sun gets up.

MARIE: Well . . . you're all right. You've got yours.

HARRY: You'd be better off in bra and pants.

MARIE: Aye aye!

HARRY: You'd probably be better covered than in a costume.

MARIE: We'll be OK.

(*Pause.*)

TIM: See how you feel after . . .

(TIM *oils himself.*)

(BELLA *watches.*)

(HARRY *and* MARIE *are lying back.*)

BELLA: Does that make you go brown?

TIM: The oil? It helps. Mainly it stops you going sore.

BELLA: I never go brown.

TIM: Put some of this on.

(BELLA *dabs herself with the oil.*)

You better put plenty on. You need it with a pale skin.

BELLA: How did you get so brown?

TIM: From me dad . . . Abdul.

BELLA: Honest . . . I never go brown.

TIM: What do you go?

BELLA: Pink and horrible.

TIM: Never mind . . . today you'll go brown and beautiful.

BELLA: Some hope.

(BELLA *dabs her stockings as* MARIE *did.*)

(TIM *watches.*)

TIM: You go brown more quickly if you go in the water.

BELLA: I can't swim.

TIM: You can paddle.

BELLA: And get soaked.

TIM: Take your clothes off.

MARIE: Aye aye aye aye!

BELLA: Can you swim?

TIM: Like an eel.

BELLA: Can you?

TIM: Want me to teach you?

MARIE: Aye aye aye aye!

27

TIM: Come on . . . I'll show you . . .

BELLA: I'm not going in.

TIM: You don't have to go in.

BELLA: I'm dead beat.

TIM: Come on . . . (*he stands and takes her hand*).

BELLA: Honest . . . I'm aching . . .

TIM: This'll revive you.

MARIE: I bet it will!

BELLA: You only just put the oil on.

TIM: I'll show you the movements . . .

MARIE: Aye aye aye aye!

TIM (*prissy*): She's only jealous.

BELLA (*rising*): I dunno . . .

HARRY (*solicitous*): Will you be OK, mate?

TIM: I guess so.

HARRY: Want me to come with you?

TIM: I'll shout if I get into trouble.

HARRY: Don't let yourself get carried away, now.

TIM: Will you be all right here?

    (TIM *glances sideways at* MARIE.)

MARIE: Cheeky sod!

HARRY (*brave*): Don't worry about me.

TIM: I'll be listening.

HARRY (*prissy*): Oh, will you?

    (TIM *picks up the beachball and throws it to* BELLA.)

TIM: Catch.

    (BELLA *misses it.*)

    Butterfingers!

    (BELLA *picks up the ball and hits* TIM *with it as he stoops.*)

BELLA: Catch. (*She laughs.*)

    (BELLA *runs off.* TIM *picks up the ball, follows.*)

    (*Sound of shouting for a moment, then silence.* MARIE *goes to the top of the dune and looks down. Then she comes back and sits by* HARRY, *who is lying on his back with his eyes closed. She looks at him. After a while she fiddles with the transistor.*)

    (*She eats another orange and takes a swig of the lemonade.*)

    (HARRY *opens his eyes.*)

HARRY: I wish you'd shut up and let's have a kip.

MARIE (*laughing*): Kip off!
> (MARIE *stretches out on the other side of the blanket.*)

HARRY: Sweet dreams.
> (*Pause. The transistor is very loud.* MARIE *lies on her back with her eyes closed.* HARRY *sits up and scrutinizes her, then lies back. After a moment he sits up again, restlessly, and again looks* MARIE *up and down.*)
>
> (*He takes a sip of lemonade.*)
>
> (*Then he goes to the top of the dune and looks around. Comes back down and lies next to* MARIE.)
>
> (*He takes her hand.*)
>
> (*She moves her hand away.*)
>
> (*He lowers the transistor. Lies back. After a minute of silence he begins to whistle and snore, at first quietly, then wildly and loudly.*)

MARIE (*laughing*): Jesus!

HARRY: Go asleep.

MARIE: I'm trying to go asleep.

HARRY: You keep waking me up just when I'm drifting off.

MARIE: Oh, I'm sorry.
> (*They close their eyes. After a silence,* HARRY *resumes his frantic whistling and snoring.*)

Christ!

HARRY: What's the matter?

MARIE: Ever tried sleeping on your side?

HARRY (*drawls*): What a super idea.
> (HARRY *turns on his side, now facing* MARIE, *very close to her.*)

MARIE: Hey up!
> (MARIE *edges away a little.*)

HARRY: You're off the blanket.

MARIE: I'm all right . . .

HARRY: Lie on the blanket . . . you'll get fulla sand.

MARIE (*moving nearer*): I'm all right now . . .

HARRY (*pulling her nearer*): You're not properly on . . .

MARIE: I'm all right now.
> (HARRY *reaches across her, tugs the blanket, and then pulls* MARIE *toward him. He tries to kiss her.*)
>
> (*Pushing back.*) Sod off!

HARRY (*sincere tone*): All I want is some sex off you.

MARIE (*laughing*): Cheeky bugger!

(MARIE *pushes him away, and lies back, with her eyes closed.*)

(HARRY *looks at her legs, then leans forward and moans.*)

What are you doing now?

HARRY: Looking up your frock.

MARIE: Bugger!

(MARIE *pulls her skirt tight around her legs.*)

HARRY (*mock-peevish*): Oh you . . . spoilsport!

MARIE: Shouldn't be peeping.

HARRY: I wasn't peeping . . . I was staring. (*Pause.*) You've got lovely legs. I like to look up them.

MARIE (*dry*): Oh . . . thanks very much.

HARRY: Now I can't see a thing.

(HARRY *slides back alongside her and stares at her neck and sweater.*)

MARIE: Gerroff!

HARRY: I can just see the top of your bra.

MARIE: Can you?

HARRY (*drawls*): Makes me feel quite horny, really.

MARIE: You make me feel naked.

HARRY (*brightly*): Why not strip off?

MARIE: Aye aye!

HARRY: You'll feel better.

MARIE: I wanna have a doze . . .

HARRY: Go on . . .

MARIE: Are you gonna behave?

HARRY: Go on . . . you have a doze . . .

MARIE: I feel as if I could drop right off.

HARRY (*leering*): I'll watch over you, darling.

MARIE (*laughing*): Oh sure!

HARRY: Go on . . .

MARIE: You lie down there . . .

(MARIE *points to a spot alongside her on the blanket.* HARRY *lies down, very obediently.*)

HARRY: Here?

MARIE: Yeah.

(MARIE *closes her eyes.*)

(HARRY *closes his.*)
(*After a moment he begins to stroke his foot against hers.*)
Stop it. You're tickling.
HARRY (*prissy*): Oh I'm sorry about that.
MARIE: Go asleep.
    (HARRY *lies back. Then he sits up again, plucks a blade of grass and begins tickling her face with it.*)
    SHUH!
HARRY: Did that tickle?
MARIE: Lay off . . . I'm dead beat.
HARRY: Close your eyes . . .
    (MARIE *closes her eyes.*)
    (HARRY *leans forward with his face only inches from hers.*)
    (*After a moment she opens her eyes and jumps.*)
MARIE: OH!
HARRY: Relax . . .
MARIE: With two blue big eyes staring into me. . . ?
HARRY (*very intense tone*): You know . . . you're lovely.
MARIE (*smiling*): Oh aye . . .
HARRY: Is your hair dyed?
MARIE: No . . . it's genuine red.
HARRY: I love you.
MARIE (*surprised, smiling*): Eh?
HARRY (*urgent*): Give us a kiss.
    (*He kisses her cheeks, lightly. She turns her face away.*)
MARIE: Gerroff!
HARRY (*mock-surprise*): Don't *you* love me?
MARIE: Oh aye!
HARRY (*smug*): Madly?
MARIE: Oh aye . . . ever since I first saw you.
HARRY (*smug*): That's what they all say.
MARIE: Conceited sod.
HARRY: I'm absolutely crazy about you.
MARIE: Are you, lad?
HARRY: I love you.
MARIE (*laughs*): Do you?
HARRY (*ardent*): Yeah.
MARIE: Forever?

HARRY: Forever now.

MARIE (*pushing him*): Gerroff . . . you're all sweaty.

HARRY (*groaning*): I'm burning with lust!

MARIE: You better go and see your mate.

HARRY: Give us a kiss.

(*They kiss lightly, then more urgently.*)

MARIE: Your face is all sandy.

HARRY: Wipe it off.

(MARIE *wipes the sand off. They lie close.*)

Listen.

MARIE: What?

HARRY: Can't you hear it?

MARIE: Hear what?

HARRY: Close your eyes and listen.

(MARIE *closes her eyes.* HARRY *sits up, looking at her.*)

MARIE: I can't hear anything.

HARRY: Concentrate.

(HARRY *lifts her skirt to her waist. She jumps away, annoyed but giggling.*)

Listen. The tide's coming in.

MARIE: Dirty bugger!

HARRY (*injured*): I only wanted to look at your legs.

MARIE: Lay off.

HARRY (*pleading*): Go on . . .

MARIE: Sod off!

HARRY: Lend us a feel till Friday.

MARIE: Feel yourself.

HARRY: Come here.

(MARIE *sits facing him.*)

(*Coy.*) Do you fancy a bit?

MARIE: I fancy a bit of peace.

HARRY: Let's go and lie down.

MARIE: Lie down where?

HARRY: Over there. It's too hot here.

MARIE: Over where?

(HARRY *kisses her passionately. He half rises, takes her hand.*)

HARRY: Come on.

MARIE (*resisting*): Where are we going?

HARRY: Over there . . . the trees.

MARIE: Let's stay here.

HARRY: It's too hot.

MARIE: You're too hot.

HARRY: We can lie down in the shade.

MARIE: No . . . come here.

(MARIE *kisses him.*)

HARRY: What's the matter?

MARIE: Nothing.

HARRY: Let's go and lie in the shade . . .

MARIE: Maybe *they're* in the shade now . . .

HARRY: Well . . . we'll share the shade.

MARIE: Nooo. . . .

HARRY: Why?

(MARIE *kisses him. Smiles at him.* HARRY *looks at her. Holds her hand. Silence.*)

MARIE: You've got nice eyes.

HARRY: I won't rape you.

MARIE: Oh well I won't go.

HARRY (*laughs*): Come on . . .

MARIE: You don't give up . . .

HARRY: Don't you trust me?

MARIE (*giggling*): I trust you . . .

HARRY: What?

MARIE: I don't trust myself.

(HARRY *lies beside her. He touches her sweater. She puts her hand over his.*)

(*He tries to slip his hand underneath but she stops him. They stay locked for a moment.*)

NO!

HARRY: I only want to feel your tits.

MARIE: Somehow I guessed.

HARRY: It's all right.

MARIE: What?

HARRY: What's wrong?

MARIE: Nothing.

HARRY: You're very well built.

MARIE: Somebody'll come.

HARRY: Let's go over there . . .

MARIE: No.

> (HARRY *tugs her, teasingly.* MARIE *pulls away.*)
> (*He falls on her and they wrestle.* MARIE *grabs his hands.*)
> Lay off!
> (HARRY *presses her down with his weight and bites her neck.*
> *She struggles but is trapped.*)
> OW!

HARRY (*biting*): Mmmmmmm.

MARIE: *Stop biting!* Ow! BUGGER!

> (HARRY *frees her and she squints to see the bite.*)

HARRY (*proud*): That'll really come up.

MARIE: That hurt like hell.

HARRY: You're branded.

MARIE: Can you see it over the sweater?

HARRY: Oh yes.

MARIE (*adjusting the sweater*): Can you?

HARRY: A dirty big red lovebite.

MARIE (*giggling*): You bastard.

> (*She slaps him lightly.*)
> (HARRY *pushes her down again.*)

HARRY: Let's go into the woods.

MARIE: You go.

HARRY: I'll eat you all up.

> (HARRY *bites her again.*)

MARIE: I'll scratch.

> (HARRY *ignores her.*)
> (*She scratches his cheek and he jumps back.*)

HARRY: OW! BITCH!

MARIE (*pleased*): I *warned* you.

HARRY (*squinting*): Does it look bad?

MARIE: It's bleeding.

HARRY: Lick it.

MARIE: Gerroff!

HARRY: Lick it.

> (HARRY *shoves his face towards hers and they wrestle.* BELLA
> *comes to the top of the dune and watches, casually.*)
> (HARRY *sees her and frees a hand to wave. They wrestle.*)

(MARIE *sees* BELLA.)

MARIE: Help! Bella . . . get this bugger off. He's eating me.

BELLA (*coming down*): Who's eating who?

HARRY: I've been assaulted.

(*The girls push* HARRY *away. He lies back on the blanket.*)

Thanks, Bella. You were just in time.

BELLA: For what?

HARRY: She was tearing me to bits.

MARIE: Bugger!

BELLA: They're both as bad.

HARRY: What?

MARIE: Eh?

BELLA: Him . . . and his mate.

(*Pause.*)

HARRY (*tough guy tone*): I hope you haven't . . . done anything
. . . to my mate . . .

BELLA: I left him tied to a tree.

HARRY: Poor Tim.

BELLA (*laughs*): I think he'll live.

MARIE (*showing the bites*): Look what this bastard did to me.

BELLA: Look at this.

(BELLA *points to her own bites.*)

(*The girls compare.*)

MARIE: Think it'll show tomorrow?

BELLA: Looks like.

MARIE: The bastard . . . I bet it'll go all purple.

BELLA: Do you think this'll show?

MARIE: Let's see . . .

BELLA: He didn't half hurt . . .

MARIE: Very nasty.

BELLA: Its gonna turn into a real bruise . . .

MARIE: What'll they say in work?

BELLA: You'll have to wear a high neck.

HARRY (*prissy*): And what about me with me face torn to bits? I
daren't face me friends. What'll all the fellers say?

MARIE: You came back just in time, Bel.

BELLA: I was waiting over there.

HARRY (*mock indignant*): *Spying* on us.

35

(TIM *enters. He struggles toward* HARRY.)

TIM (*choked voice*): Gawd . . .

HARRY (*high-pitched*): Tim!

TIM: Harry!

HARRY: You . . . made it back . . .

TIM: It's good to see you . . . mate . . .

HARRY: You made it back.

TIM: Shucks . . .

HARRY: Was it . . . rough?

TIM (*turns away*): I'd rather not . . . talk about it.

HARRY: No . . . no. (*Pause.*) Was it rough?

TIM: Ahhhhhhh.

HARRY: Are you all right?

TIM (*choked*): Don't worry . . . about . . . me.

HARRY: I understand.

TIM: One thing . . .

HARRY: What? What?

TIM: One thing I want to ask you . . .

HARRY: Anything.

(*The two men stare intently at each other, ignoring the girls completely. The girls stare intently at the men.*)

What?

TIM: I realize I have no right to ask this . . .

HARRY: Ask me. Ask me anything.

(*Pause.*)

TIM: Did you get your hole?

HARRY: No.

(*Pause.*)

Did you?

TIM: No.

(*The men look commiseratingly at each other.*)

Never mind . . . mate.

HARRY: Not worth torturing yourself . . .

TIM: You know what they are.

HARRY: They're just . . . (*waves his hand*).

TIM: They're just a couple of prickteasers.

HARRY: That's it.

MARIE: You what?

36

HARRY: That's what they are . . .

TIM: Prickteasers.

MARIE: What?

BELLA: Prickwhat?

HARRY: PRICK-TEASERS!

(*Both girls have a fit of giggling and laughing.*)

MARIE: Dirty buggers!

BELLA: Prickteasers!

MARIE: They use some lovely language.

BELLA: Cheeky buggers!

MARIE (*convulsed*): Prickteasers!

(*The men lie down on the blanket.*)

TIM: Gawd . . . I'm exhausted.

HARRY: Have a kip. I'll keep watch.

MARIE (*to* BELLA): You all right?

BELLA: Just about.

MARIE: Did you learn to swim?

BELLA: HA HA.

HARRY (*to* TIM): Have a buttie.

TIM: Thanks. Are you having one?

HARRY: I'm having an orange.

(*The girls suddenly look at each other and go off into a fit of giggling again.*)

MARIE: I'm going over there . . .

BELLA: Oh.

MARIE: Are you gonna hold my hand?

BELLA: Yeah . . . I'll come with you.

(*They head off towards the woods, still giggling.*)

HARRY: Where are you going?

MARIE: For a piss.

(*The girls exit.*)

HARRY (*queer tone*): FOR A PISS!

(HARRY *and* TIM *sit looking at each other.*)

(*Silence.*)

(HARRY *jumps up to the top of the dune.*)

(*Laughs.*) And the waters covered the earth . . .

(*He comes down and lies by* TIM.)

(*Silence.*)

TIM: Jesus!

HARRY: Yeah . . .

TIM: What time is it?

HARRY: About ten o'clock.

TIM: Only ten o'clock . . .

HARRY: I know . . .

(*Silence.*)

TIM: The state of them.

HARRY: Notice what they're wearing?

TIM: Same as last night.

HARRY: Exactly.

TIM: Wait till the sun gets up.

HARRY (*holding his nose*): Ugggghhh.

TIM: It's gonna be a scorcher, too.

(*Silence.*)

HARRY: All they did was put fresh paint on.

TIM: The van stunk this morning.

HARRY: I had the fan on.

TIM: Yeah . . . it was blowing a gale.

HARRY: The stuff they put on.

TIM: No wonder they give off.

HARRY: What a bloody pong.

TIM: It's the sweat.

HARRY: And the rest . . .

(*Silence.*)

TIM (*wry laugh*): Last night was great.

HARRY: That was in the alehouse . . .

TIM: And after . . .

HARRY: We musta been pissed.

TIM: Seemed different then.

(*Silence.*)

HARRY (*laughs*): We'll have to stay in the friggin' water.

TIM (*laughs*): What . . . all day?

HARRY: We said we'd take them for a drink afterwards, too.

TIM: Yeah.

HARRY: Maybe we could go early . . .

TIM: How?

HARRY: Say it's to avoid the traffic?

38

TIM: How early?

HARRY: I dunno . . . four o'clock.

TIM: Another six hours.

HARRY: Jesus!

(*Silence.*)

(TIM *stares at* HARRY, *and slowly begins to grin, then chuckle.* HARRY *responds.*)

What a fucking stink.

TIM: Lovely!

HARRY: Lovely!

(*Both men lie back, laughing, holding their noses. The girls shout in the distance.*)

(TIM *gets up quickly.*)

TIM: Come on . . .

HARRY: What?

TIM (*queer tone*): D'you wanna go for a piss?

HARRY (*queer tone*): Can I hold your hand?

TIM: Come on . . . they'll be back in a minute.

HARRY (*joins him*): Right.

TIM (*laughing*): The dirty cows!

HARRY (*laughing*): The dirty cows!

(*They run off toward the beach.*)

(*Sound of the girls' voices, and pop music.*)

CURTAIN

act two

Scene: About midday. The girls lie on the blanket, MARIE *reading a paperback,* BELLA *dozing. The transistor is playing.* MARIE *is very restless. She puts the paperback down.*

MARIE: Dirty buggers!

(BELLA *doesn't respond.* MARIE *takes an orange from the bag. Swigs some lemonade. Looks at what is left in the bottle, puts the bottle back. She peels the orange, tosses the peel aside. Eats the orange. Her hands are sticky, so she rubs them on her skirt. Spits out pips.*)

(*She gets up, spins round to the music, turns up the volume.*)

(*Then she goes to the top of the dune and looks across toward the beach.*)

(*After a minute she comes back down. Another little shake to the music. She sits down, stares at* BELLA. *She leans across and taps her.*)

BELLA (*stirring*): Ehhh?

MARIE: You wanna orange?

BELLA: Oh . . . ta. . . . No, I'll have a drink.

(BELLA *takes out the bottle.*)

MARIE: Go easy . . . there's not much left.

BELLA: No . . . you've been swigging it all morning.

MARIE: Well . . .

BELLA: You have.

MARIE (*snaps*): There's sod all else to do.

(BELLA *sips, puts the bottle back.*)

BELLA: Have a sleep.

MARIE: I've had a sleep.

BELLA: Don't pick on me.

MARIE: What time is it?

BELLA: I dunno.

MARIE: Feels like we been here all bloody summer.

BELLA: Am I brown?

MARIE: Oh you're lovely . . .

(BELLA *dabs on some oil.*)

They're taking their time.

BELLA: They musta gone for a swim.

MARIE: Wish I could swim . . . hey . . . shall we go down?

BELLA: Down where?

MARIE: Down there . . . to the beach?

BELLA: You go.

MARIE: Oh aye . . .

(MARIE *goes to the top of the dune.*)

BELLA: Can you see them?

MARIE: No.

BELLA: Maybe they swam out.

MARIE: Yea . . . over to New Brighton, probably!

BELLA: Come down.

MARIE: There's no sign of them . . .

(BELLA *puts the oil away, stretches, and sprawls on her back on the blanket.*)

BELLA: They'll be back . . . come down.

(MARIE *comes down and throws herself on to the blanket. She picks up the book. Her eyes widen.*)

MARIE: This book . . . it's crazy.

BELLA: Is it?

MARIE: Yeah . . . it's . . . (*She tosses it aside. Pause.*)

BELLA: Huh?

MARIE: Do you fancy him?

BELLA: Who?

MARIE: Santa Claus! (*Silence.*) Who do you think?

BELLA: Oh . . . he's all right.

MARIE: He musta been all right last night.

BELLA (*grinning*): How do you mean?

MARIE: In the backa the van.

BELLA: He *was* all right.

(*Pause.*)

41

MARIE (*laughs*): Did you get your hole?

BELLA (*laughs*): You mean, did he get his?

MARIE: Dirty buggers!

(*Pause.*)

BELLA: Anyway . . . you were doing all right yourself . . .

MARIE: Eh?

BELLA: In the front of the van.

MARIE (*grinning*): Oh aye . . .

BELLA: They don't waste much time . . .

MARIE: They didn't last night . . . but . . .

BELLA: Yeah . . .

MARIE: I bet they've had some fun out here.

BELLA: After Saturday night.

MARIE: What?

BELLA: If they pick anything up on Saturday night.

MARIE: Oh yeah. . . . Cheeky sod!

(*Pause.*)

BELLA: That bite's going blue.

MARIE: Is it? (*Squinting.*)

BELLA: Tomorrow it'll be all purple.

MARIE: What about yours?

BELLA (*squints*): Yeah . . . (*Pulls up her sweater.*) But look at this one.

MARIE: Jesus! You wanna be careful.

BELLA: What?

MARIE: He'll bite it off.

BELLA (*laughing*): Wants his mammy.

MARIE: You musta got him real worked up.

BELLA: Doesn't take much.

MARIE (*howls with laughter*): Prickteaser!

BELLA (*laughing*): Prickteaser!

(*Both girls double up on the blanket in a fit of laughing and giggling.*)

(*They lie back.*)

Christ . . . it's hot.

MARIE: Yeah . . .

BELLA: Wish we had costumes.

MARIE: Yeah . . . I'm melting away.

BELLA: I'd give anything for a pan of cold water.

MARIE: Yeah . . . the sand sticks to you.

BELLA: I'm soaked in sweat.

MARIE: Me too.

(MARIE *gets her bag, takes out some perfume, dabs herself.*)
That's better. Want some?

BELLA: Ta.

(BELLA *dabs on some perfume.*)
(MARIE *studies herself in a mirror, puts on some make-up.*)
(BELLA *watches her, then picks up her own bag and does the same.*)

MARIE: Do I look all right?

BELLA: Dead sexy.

MARIE: Oh aye!

BELLA: You look all right.

MARIE: My hair's rotten with sand. (*Scratching.*)

BELLA (*looking in the mirror*): Does that look all right?

MARIE: It's a bit streaky.

BELLA: Yeah . . . I thought it was.

(BELLA *touches up her make-up.*)

MARIE: That looks better now.

(*Suddenly the beachball bounces into the middle of the hollow. Both girls jump back.* HARRY *appears at the top of the dune, stands for a moment, grinning, then leaps down. Fresh from the swim, he stands between the girls, shaking himself and showering them.*)
Sod off!

HARRY: Thought that would cool you down.

(HARRY *dries himself, rubbing vigorously, flexing his muscles.*)

MARIE: How was New Brighton?

HARRY: Eh? Oh . . . too crowded to stay.

MARIE: Thought you'd got drowned.

HARRY: Worried about your lift home?

BELLA: Where's your mate?

HARRY: In the woods.

BELLA (*laughing*): He wastes no time, does he? (*Gets up.*) I'll go and see what he's up to.

HARRY: I'll tell you if you really want to know.

(BELLA *goes off left.*)

(HARRY *sits down, looks in the beach bag.*)

Where's all the oranges?

MARIE (*points to peelings*): There.

HARRY: Christ . . .

MARIE: We were dying of thirst.

HARRY: What about the lemonade? (*Examines the bottle.*) You might just as well have finished it off.

MARIE: I will if you like.

HARRY: I believe you.

MARIE: There's some butties left.

HARRY: Thanks very much!

(HARRY *takes a sip of the lemonade and eats a sandwich.*)

MARIE: There was sod all to do.

HARRY: Huh.

MARIE: You were gone ages.

HARRY: We had a good swim.

MARIE: Wish I could swim.

HARRY: You shoulda brought a costume.

MARIE: I haven't *got* a costume.

(*Pause.* HARRY *eats his sandwich. Fiddles with the transistor.*)

HARRY (*sourly*): WONDERFUL RADIO ONE!

MARIE: What's the matter with it?

HARRY: That's the fifteenth time the D.J.'s played that brand new number. He must puke whenever he puts it on. (*Pause.*) It's OK once, but fifteen times!

MARIE: It hasn't been on fifteen times.

HARRY: Well, ten times, seven times, whatever it is. Maybe that's why they keep changing the D.J.'s—because they don't change the tunes.

(HARRY *finishes the sandwich, licks his lips.*)

HARRY: Now it's my turn to die of thirst.

MARIE (*leaning toward him*): I'll give you a big sloppy kiss . . . that'll help your thirst.

HARRY: What? A mouthful of spit?

MARIE: It's nice.

HARRY: I'd rather suck me thumb.

(HARRY *sits sucking his thumb.*)

44

MARIE: Poor little baby.

(HARRY—*sucking sounds.*)

MARIE (*pushing her breasts out*): Wanna drop of milk?

HARRY: I only drink sterilized.

(*They sit for a moment.*)

(BELLA *returns.*)

MARIE: Where is he?

BELLA: In the woods.

MARIE: Did you find him?

BELLA: Yeah.

(BELLA *sits. She looks at* HARRY.)

What's he doing?

MARIE: Sucking his thumb. (*Pause.*) Where is he then?

BELLA: He was sitting under a tree.

MARIE: Oh.

BELLA: I asked him what he was doing. He just looked at me.
So I came back.

HARRY: He was probably having a crap.

BELLA: With his costume on?

HARRY: He's very modest.

(*Pause.*)

MARIE: Whose is the book?

HARRY: What book?

MARIE: This one . . . it was in the van.

HARRY: Somebody musta left it in the van.

MARIE: Wonder who?

HARRY: Have you read it?

MARIE: Bits of it.

HARRY: Like it?

MARIE (*giggles*): It's a scream.

HARRY (*indignant tone*): It's a well-known Indian sex manual.

MARIE: Yeah . . . a dirty book.

HARRY: What's dirty about it?

MARIE: I prefer sex the English way.

HARRY: Christ . . . a patriot!

(TIM *returns and sits by* HARRY.)

TIM: Pass us an orange.

HARRY: It's the last one.

TIM: I'll give you a slice.
> (HARRY *passes the orange*.)
> Any lemonade?
HARRY: Just a drop.
> (HARRY *passes the lemonade*. TIM *drains it*.)
MARIE: Shoulda brought some more.
TIM (*to* HARRY): How much did you have?
HARRY: Just a swig.
TIM: So did I.
HARRY: We had three bottles this morning.
TIM: How many oranges did you have?
HARRY: Two.
TIM: I only had one.
MARIE: You had two.
TIM: You had ten.
MARIE: I was thirsty.
TIM: Greedy cow!
HARRY: You've been at it all day.
MARIE: What do you want me to do? Run and fetch some more?
TIM: Any butties left?
HARRY: No. All gone.
MARIE: You had your share.
TIM: I'm dying for a drink.
> (*Pause*.)
HARRY: D'you wanna go . . . get a drink on the way?
> (*Pause*.)
MARIE: What time is it?
HARRY: About half twelve.
MARIE: It's early.
TIM: Pubs'll be open till two.
MARIE: You mean go and come back?
TIM: Could do . . .
HARRY: Not much time . . .
TIM: Gotta get away early, though . . . avoid the jams.
HARRY: Yeah.
> (*Silence*.)
BELLA: I wanna get some tan in.
MARIE: Yeah.

46

BELLA (*to* TIM): Am I brown?

TIM: You're all pink and horrible.

BELLA: Thanks very much!

TIM: You said you would be.

BELLA: You said I wouldn't.

TIM (*wry*): Wrong again.

> (BELLA *grimaces, lies back.* TIM *does the same. Pause.* MARIE *takes a blade of grass and traces it across* HARRY's *face.*)

MARIE: You wore out?

HARRY: Yeah.

MARIE: It's the sun.

HARRY: Huh.

MARIE: Wanna go in the shade?

HARRY: I wanna go asleep.

MARIE: You could go asleep . . .

HARRY: Oh yeah . . .

> (MARIE *climbs to the top of the dune, looks around, comes back to* HARRY.)

MARIE: Like a desert island.

HARRY: Waiting for a ship.

MARIE: Yeah. (*Pause.*) Is this where you come to do your courting?

HARRY: No, this is where we come to do our fucking.

MARIE (*laughs*): You coulda fooled me.

HARRY: We do our courting in the alehouse.

MARIE: Like last night?

HARRY: That's right.

MARIE: Where?

HARRY: Eh?

MARIE: D'you go in the woods?

HARRY: They're fulla flies and dogshit.

> (HARRY *turns and lies on his stomach with his eyes closed.*)

MARIE: Ooohhh . . . look at all the little curly hairs sticking out.

HARRY: Bugger off.

> (MARIE *pats him. Plucks a hair.* HARRY *jumps.*)
> OW!

MARIE: Big baby.

HARRY (*twists away*): Lay off.

(MARIE *fiddles with the transistor.*)

MARIE: Let's have a dance . . . (*She stands dancing by herself.*)

HARRY: You have a dance.

MARIE: Come on . . .

HARRY: I'm too tired.

MARIE: Go asleep then.

HARRY: I'm trying . . . I'm trying.

(MARIE *throws a towel over his head. He lets it lie there.*)

MARIE (*to* BELLA): How's lover boy?

BELLA: Flaked out.

MARIE: Let's have a dance.

BELLA: Make a change.

(MARIE *turns the transistor full blast, and the girls dance.*
MARIE *kicks the towel away from* HARRY. *They dance across
the men.*)

MARIE: They can't dance.

BELLA: No?

MARIE: Only with each other.

BELLA: Probably.

MARIE: I wonder who leads.

(*The girls laugh and giggle.*)

Christ . . . I'm sweating.

BELLA (*wriggling*): So am I . . . soaked.

MARIE: Just think . . . we coulda been dancing at the Cavern
now instead of the bloody sandhills.

BELLA: Yeah.

MARIE: See the talent.

BELLA: Yeah.

MARIE: Mind you, we'd probably be sweating worse.

BELLA: I wouldn't mind.

MARIE: Me neither.

(MARIE *kicks sand over* HARRY.)

HARRY: Bugger you!

MARIE: Jesus, it's alive!

(*The girls lie down.*)

BELLA (*pulling at her pants*): The sand gets in everything.

MARIE: It's a menace.

BELLA: It's all right for *them*.

48

HARRY: You shoulda brought costumes.

MARIE: I'd rather go to New Brighton Baths.

HARRY: HAHAHA!

MARIE: What are you laughing at?

HARRY: When did you ever go to the baths?

MARIE: I've been there often.

HARRY: Prefer that, do you?

MARIE: Yeah. (*Then ignoring him, turns to* BELLA.) You can have more laughs at the baths, anyway.

BELLA: You can have more laughs at the morgue!

MARIE: Bloody right.

> (*Pause.* BELLA *leans back.* MARIE *looks round, restless. Strokes the sand with her hand. She tries to pile it up.*)
>
> (*Childish.*) You can't even build a bloody sandcastle . . . the sand's no good.

BELLA: The sand's too fine.

> (*Long pause.* MARIE *filters the sand through her fingers.* BELLA *watches. The men lie with eyes closed. The sun belts down. The transistor is off. Distant sound of ships' sirens.*)

MARIE (*looking at the men*): Look at them . . . the ravers.

BELLA: Huh . . . the jet set.

MARIE: Big build-up.

BELLA: Mouth.

MARIE: All mouth.

BELLA: Can't half talk.

MARIE: Yeah.

BELLA: We'll have to find somewhere else to drink.

MARIE: Plenty of places.

BELLA: Start next week.

MARIE: Yeah.

> (*Pause.*)
>
> Mind you . . . I think these were in the wrong pub.

BELLA: Got mis-directed?

MARIE (*laughs*): Lost their way.

> (*Pause.*)
>
> (*Mimicking*): Passsss ussss an orange.

BELLA (*mimicking*): Ssssave ussss a ssslice.

MARIE: Wonder who's the giver?

(*Both girls burst out laughing.*)

No . . . you know what they are really?

BELLA: Go on . . .

MARIE: A couple of . . . cunt-teasers.

BELLA (*laughing*): Cunt-teasers?

MARIE: You know . . . a couple of cunt-teasers.

(*The girls fall about laughing.* HARRY *looks at them.*)

Know what you are? Cunt-teasers!

HARRY: You should know.

MARIE: Eh.

HARRY: I bet yours has got cobwebs on it.

MARIE: If I waited for you!

(*Both girls howl and roll about laughing.* HARRY *stares and then slings the beach ball at* MARIE. *She hurls it back at him. It bounces away.* BELLA *picks it up. Throws it to* MARIE. MARIE *throws it back.* BELLA *punches it back, wide.* MARIE *collects it, comes behind* HARRY, *bounces the ball on his stomach.*)

Come on.

HARRY: Eh?

MARIE: You gonna play?

HARRY: Frig off?

MARIE: Thought you was the athletic type?

HARRY (*pointing at her breasts*): Where did you get them? Outa the catalogue?

MARIE (*laughing, bouncing*). They're all meat, lad.

(MARIE *throws the ball to* BELLA. *The girls jump around, across the men, the pace getting faster.*)

(MARIE *stops, peels off her stockings, flourishes them and tosses them over* HARRY.)

HARRY (*disgusted*): Bitch!

(HARRY *flings the stockings aside, rolls away.* BELLA *takes off her stockings, throws them at* TIM. *He rolls away.* MARIE *hitches her skirt at her waist.* BELLA *does the same.*)

(MARIE *feints to hurl the ball at* HARRY. *He flinches. She howls with laughter, tosses the ball to* BELLA. *The girls leap around, now slinging the ball at each other.*)

(MARIE *throws the ball at* HARRY *and catches him hard on the face. He yelps.*)

HARRY: OW! BITCH!

MARIE (*laughing*): Oh! Very sorry!

> (*The ball bounces off toward* TIM. *He tries to grab it but* BELLA *intercepts it.* TIM *tackles her, but she avoids him and tosses it to* MARIE. HARRY *grabs it, feints to throw it to* TIM *but swivels and slings it hard at* MARIE. *She ducks and the ball bounces and flies off toward the woods.*)
>
> (*Pause.*)
>
> (TIM *and* BELLA *stand transfixed on the left, nearer the woods. Centre stands* MARIE. HARRY *stands, slightly higher, on the slope, on the right.*)
>
> (MARIE *turns round, looks at* BELLA, *turns back to face* HARRY.)
>
> (*Silence.*)

HARRY: Fetch it.

MARIE: You threw it.

HARRY: At you.

MARIE: Huh!

> (*Pause.*)

HARRY: Fetch it.

MARIE: Sod off!

> (*Pause.*)
>
> (BELLA *turns towards the woods,* TIM *siezes her.*)

BELLA (*struggling*): Leggo.

TIM: Stay there.

BELLA: I'll fetch it.

TIM: You won't.

> (HARRY *comes down toward* MARIE.)

HARRY: Fetch it.

MARIE: Sod off . . . it was you threw it. (*Pause.*) Fetch it yourself.

> (HARRY *lifts his hand as if to hit her. She cowers back then stands.*)

BELLA: I'll get the bloody ball.

> (TIM *holds her.*)

HARRY: FETCH IT!

> (MARIE *doesn't move.* HARRY *tries to push her towards the woods. She sits suddenly so that he falls across her. She*

51

laughs, throwing her head back and howling.)
(HARRY *straddles her.*)
(*He scoops up a handful of sand and pours some into her mouth. She gags, splutters, struggles, but* HARRY *holds her down. He pours sand over her face.*)

BELLA: You BASTARD!

(BELLA *jumps forward, is held back by* TIM.)

TIM: Shut your mouth.

BELLA: Sod off!

TIM: You want the same? Shut your mouth.

(MARIE *lies with her mouth and eyes tight closed as* HARRY *pours the sand on to her face. She struggles to avoid it but is tightly held.*)
(HARRY *empties his hand, scoops up another handful, holds it poised above her face.*)
(*Pause.*)

HARRY: You gonna fetch the ball now?

(MARIE *opens her eyes, blinking painfully, stares at* HARRY.)
(*She spits in his mouth. He falls to the side and she kicks him between the legs and scrambles away.*)
(HARRY *lies on his knees, propping himself up with one hand, spitting violently into the sand and retching and rubbing his mouth with his free hand, in agony.*)
(MARIE *sits.*)
(TIM *steps forward, then stops.*)
(BELLA *breaks free, goes off, comes back in a second with the ball. She tosses it toward* HARRY.)

BELLA: There's your ball.

(BELLA *sits down by* MARIE, *whispers with her.* HARRY *is still clearing his throat and spitting. When he stops he sits and looks at* TIM. TIM *stands separate from the others.*)
(*Pause.*)
(TIM *walks forward, picks up the ball and throws it hard at* MARIE *from close range. It hits her on the head and she yelps.*)

TIM: Gonna play?

MARIE: Bugger off!

(MARIE's *eyes are wet from the stinging pain of the sand, and now the ball. She throws the ball away, wildly.*)

52

(TIM *collects it, gives it to* HARRY.)

(HARRY *holds it for a second, looks at* TIM, *takes careful aim at* MARIE *and hits her hard with it on the body.*)

(MARIE *scrambles away.*)

(BELLA *tries to intercept the ball but* TIM *picks it up, takes aim at* MARIE.)

(MARIE *runs to the right, is barred by* HARRY. TIM *hits her hard with it on the back. She falls down.*)

(BELLA *collects the ball.* HARRY *forces it from her.* HARRY *hits* MARIE *on the head with the ball. She sprawls over, scrambles up, hops towards the left, is barred by* TIM. *He feints to hit her with the ball, she shrinks back.* BELLA *jumps in front of him.*)

TIM: You want it?

(BELLA *stands her ground.*)

(TIM *hits her in the face with the ball. She cries, claps her hand to her face, sits.*)

BELLA (*moans*): Stop it . . . stop it!

(*Pause.*)

(*The ball has rolled centre stage, between* HARRY *and* MARIE. HARRY *steps toward it.* MARIE *steps back, hands up protecting herself.*)

(HARRY *stops, looks at* MARIE. *She looks back at him.*)

(*Pause.*)

For Christ's sake . . . stop it!

(HARRY *sits down.*)

(*Pause.*)

(MARIE *sits, wipes her face with the towel.* BELLA *sits near her, wipes her face. Their movements are very slow.* TIM *stands looking at the others.*)

(BELLA *opens her handbag, offers* MARIE *some face cream.* MARIE *takes it, opens it, dabs some on her face.* TIM *steps forward and grabs the cream.*)

TIM: Throw that muck away.

(*He looks at the cream in his hand, disgustedly, and hurls it across the dunes.*)

MARIE: What's the . . .

BELLA: He's crazy.

TIM: MUCK! MUCK! MUCK!

(TIM *seizes the open handbag. Looks in it with fascinated revulsion.* MARIE *reaches for it, half-heartedly.* TIM *ignores her.*)

BELLA: Gimme me bag.

TIM: What do you want? (*Roots in the bag.*)

BELLA: Bastard! Gimme the bag.

(TIM *begins picking out various items of make-up, holds them at finger-tip, looks at them, tosses them to the sand.* BELLA *scrambles around trying to recover them, swearing at* TIM, *sobbing, but no longer attempting to get the bag itself.*)
(HARRY *watches.*)

TIM: What do you want? Mascara? Muck! (*Throws it away.*) Nail varnish? (*Now with increasing intensity.*) Muck! What's this? Perfume? (*Takes out a small bottle, examines it, opens it. Sniffs. Looks sickened.*) 'Passionate Temptations' . . . MUCK! (*Drains the bottle in the sand.*)
These . . . what are these? Eyelashes? False eyelashes! (*Almost pleading.*) Do you . . . do you wear these? (*Intense.*) They're weird. Are they false? Or real? From some poor bastard coolie's head? Muck! Muck!
(*Throws them away . . .* BELLA *scrambles frantically for them.*)

BELLA: ME LASHES! MARIE, ME LASHES!
(*Both girls rake frantically through the sand.*)

TIM (*rooting in the bag*): You carry this filth with you. Filth! And smear it with your sweat! Muck! (*Takes out a packet with brush and powder, opens it, smells the brush, looks sick.*) What's this here? Brush-on powder . . . 'Radiant Beaches!' (*Bursts out laughing.*) Jesus! RADIANT BEACHES!
(*Throws the powder and the brush into the sand.*)

BELLA: Stop it . . . for Christ's sake . . .

TIM: 'Mediterranean Gold' . . . Suntan? That what this is? Phoney suntan? That's great. Shit! Shit to smear on your skin, shit to make you sexy, shit . . . (*Squeezes some drops from a tube of sun lotion, looks at his hand, rubs it violently.*) It's stained me. Shit! Muck! (*Hurls the tube away.*)
(BELLA *scrambles after the tube.*)

BELLA: You swine, you swine!

TIM: This bag . . . it's covered in muck! Look at it. Like you . . . covered in muck. (*Takes out a lipstick.*) What's this?

54

Lipstick? No . . . 'Lingering Kisses!' Jesus! Lingering
arseholes! Muck, more muck!
(BELLA *snatches at the lipstick.* TIM *catches her hand.*)
You want this?
(*He daubs a cross on her forehead. She wriggles away, he
holds the bag upside down and empties the contents into the
sand and tosses the bag aside.*)
BELLA (*rubbing her forehead*): You bastard . . . I'll get you . . .
MARIE: He's mad.
BELLA: Get the things . . .
(*The girls scramble around collecting the bits of make-up and
stuffing them in the bag.* TIM *stands watching.* HARRY *sits.*)
BELLA: Let's get out . . .
MARIE: Sod them . . .
BELLA: We'll get a lift.
(MARIE *reaches for her stockings, sits to put them on.* BELLA
reaches for hers. TIM *steps forward, picks them up. Pushes*
BELLA *back.*)
Gimme them.
(TIM *holds the stockings dangling.*)
TIM: Do these burn?
BELLA: Gimme me stockings, you bastard!
TIM (*to* HARRY): Matches.
(HARRY *gives him a lighter.*)
(TIM *waves the lighter near the foot of the stocking.* BELLA
makes a grab. HARRY *pushes her back.*)
(*Threatening with the lighter.*) I'll burn you. Burn you, too.
BELLA: Don't burn them . . . please.
TIM: You reek.
BELLA: Please don't burn them.
TIM: You reek of piss . . . and powder.
MARIE: Let's go . . . never mind them.
(HARRY *stops her.*)
(TIM *stands holding the stocking, with the lighter lit, waving it.*
He speaks in alternating tones of horror and derision,
sometimes, laughing absurdly at his story.)
TIM: That smell . . . is familiar. (*Laughs.*) Years ago I painted a
ladies' lavatory. Yeah . . . a lavo in a club in Slater Street.

That was a job I didn't forget . . .

You musta know the place . . . in Slater Street. They had a downstairs lavo for the men and an upstairs for the birds . . . only the birds could go up the stairs. Remember? You remember, Harry?

HARRY: I remember.

TIM: I don't remember the name . . . anyway, that was the place. I went up there . . . one Sunday . . . went up the stairs to paint the lavo. As I was going up the stairs I began to . . . began to smell it. This sickening smell . . . I got up the stairs, went through into this little room on the left. There was a dirty little washbowl . . . no water, I tried it . . . and this bloody great mirror on the wall. And the place stunk . . . I tried to force the window, it wouldn't open.

The lavatory was in the corner. The door was open, you couldn't lock it. I went in there. Jesus! It stunk of cunt and . . . scent. And the strongest was the scent! It smelt . . . sweet . . . made me dizzy . . . I sat down . . . yeah . . . (*laughing*) I had to sit down on the po! It was dark in there . . .

I thought I was gonna be sick.

There were holes in the door and in the walls. Little holes drilled through the wood . . . maybe picked with nail files . . . little spy holes . . . for the birds piping . . . And there was this thing on the floor . . . a rag someone had left there . . . a jamrag . . . left it on the floor of the lavatory!

So . . . so I sat there for a while . . . with that stench . . . I tried to breathe through my nose. And I thought of the birds all collecting up there from the dance downstairs, standing in front of that bloody great mirror, covering themselves with muck . . . and the dust in the washbasin . . . and us . . .

. . . us blokes waiting downstairs for the little angels!

In the end I went and stood in front of the mirror, I looked at meself in the mirror . . . I started laughing. Yeah. I laughed. I wanted to go out and stop all the men in the street and tell them what I had just seen . . . maybe bring them back up, give them a look at it . . . I thought what they'd say . . . I was crying with laughter . . . bloody hilarious. I couldn't stop.

Then I felt different. Then it didn't . . . matter, didn't affect me any more. I opened the door of the lavo, got me things out . . .

The walls of the lavo were covered in . . . words. You know . . . just like ours . . . just the same . . .

'LICK ME OUT, BABY'

'MY BROTHER FEELS ME . . .'

'MEET ME HERE AT . . .'

(TIM *falters. Looks at the stocking. Re-lights the lighter.*)

There was no water in the cistern either. The po was all bunged up . . . up near the top. They just kept using it.

BELLA: Gimme that . . .

TIM: I covered it all in bright orange paint.

(*Pause.*)

BELLA: Gimme that stocking.

TIM: You reek. (*With loathing.*) You stink of sweat . . . and scent. You oughta be scrubbed with wire wool. You oughta be scraped-down. If I had a blow-lamp now!

(TIM *burns the stocking. Nobody else moves.*)

BELLA (*sobbing*): Bastard!

(TIM *burns the other stocking.*)

MARIE: Let's get back . . .

(MARIE *picks up her bag.* TIM *seizes it, throws it to* HARRY. HARRY *holds it.* BELLA *lunges for it.*)

BELLA: *Oh, not that too!*

TIM (*seizing her*): You reek. (*Tears at her skirt.*)

BELLA (*screaming*): Leggo of me. Bastard.

TIM: I'm gonna scrub the muck off you.

(TIM *forces her toward the beach.*)

HARRY (*to* MARIE): You too.

MARIE: Please . . .

(MARIE *makes a run.* HARRY *jumps after her. They struggle. He pulls her up and forces her towards the beach.*)

CURTAIN

57

act three

Scene: Now about six o'clock, the light fading a little. HARRY *is on his knees, searching through the sand. After a minute,* BELLA *enters from left. She is wrapped in a blanket.*

HARRY: Hi!
BELLA: Hi!
    (BELLA *sits. She watches* HARRY *searching.*)
HARRY: They've vanished.
BELLA: Hey?
HARRY: The lashes . . . they've vanished.
    (*Pause.* BELLA *watches* HARRY *combing the sand.*)
    I'm probably burying them.
BELLA: You'll never find a pair of lashes in the sand.
HARRY: Don't be too sure . . .
    (*Pause.* HARRY *carries on searching.*)
BELLA: They don't matter . . .
HARRY: Don't they?
BELLA: It's not worth the bother . . .
HARRY: Listen. . . . Once, we were driving back from here. And one of the girls lost a contact lens. I mean . . . she dropped it in the car . . .
BELLA (*laughing*): She *dropped* it?
HARRY: Well . . . she lost it in the car.
BELLA: Front or back?
HARRY: Eh?
BELLA: Front or back?
HARRY: Front or back . . . well . . .
BELLA: Were you driving?

HARRY: Yeah . . . anyway . . . she dropped these lenses . . . I
    mean, she dropped a lenses . . . a lens . . .
BELLA: How?
HARRY: She was sitting in the back. All I know is, she suddenly
    screamed out, I've lost me lens!
BELLA: The way you tell a story!
HARRY: So I climbed into the back . . . and (*now lamely*) . . .
    anyway I found her lens.
BELLA: Sorry . . .
HARRY: What?
BELLA: Did I spoil your story?
HARRY: No . . . no.
    (HARRY *carries on searching*.)
    (BELLA *lies back*.)
    (HARRY *picks something up from the sand, and examines it*.)
HARRY: Hey!
BELLA: What?
HARRY: What's this?
    (BELLA *takes it from him*.)
BELLA (*laughing*): A brush.
HARRY: I know it's a brush . . . what is it?
BELLA: For brushing shades on . . .
HARRY: Yours?
BELLA: Yeah.
HARRY: Oh . . . great!
BELLA: All I need now is the stuff to brush on.
HARRY: Christ! Did you lose that too?
BELLA: Yeah . . . it doesn't matter . . .
HARRY (*cautiously*): D'you use that stuff?
BELLA: Yeah.
HARRY: You don't need it.
BELLA: I can't get a tan.
HARRY (*laughing*): You don't *need* a tan.
BELLA: You prefer me pink and horrible?
HARRY: You look great without a tan . . . you're fair . ..
BELLA: So are you.
HARRY: That's different.
BELLA: Is it?

HARRY: You don't need a tan.

BELLA (*laughing*): Just as well!

(HARRY *carries on searching. He comes up with a tomato.*)

HARRY: Hey!

BELLA: What?

HARRY: Look at this!

BELLA: Food!

HARRY: Liquor!

(*Pause.*)

(HARRY *rolls the tomato down his arm, bounces it on his muscle and catches it.*)

Want it?

BELLA: D'you?

HARRY (*noble tone*): We'll save them a bit.

BELLA: Better wait.

HARRY: Yeah . . . save it till they come back.

(*Both laugh.* HARRY *sprawls near* BELLA.)

Looks like my eyelash detector has failed.

BELLA: Never mind.

HARRY: They cost much?

BELLA: A few bob.

(*Pause.*)

HARRY: You mad?

BELLA (*smiles*): No.

HARRY: Tim's all right.

BELLA: Yeah . . .

HARRY: Funny.

BELLA: He's all right.

HARRY: I don't know what happened.

BELLA: Doesn't matter.

(*Pause.*)

HARRY: He's a good mate.

BELLA: Is he?

HARRY: One of the best. (*Pause.*) The best.

BELLA: Have you known him long?

HARRY: Oh aye, I knew him when he used hair oil.

BELLA: You see a lot of each other?

HARRY: Yeah.

(*Pause.*)

BELLA: Do you . . .

HARRY: What?

BELLA: The two of you . . . do you always come here . . .

HARRY: If we pick anything . . .

BELLA: If you pick anything up on Saturday night!

HARRY: Usually.

BELLA: Do you always 'end up in the woods'?

HARRY: Not always . . .

BELLA: But usually . . .

HARRY (*prissy*): Only if we're pressed . . .

BELLA: You do that too well.

HARRY: Eh?

BELLA: You could easily be taken for a queer.

HARRY (*slightly embarrassed*): Well . . . you know better.

BELLA: You could be mistaken for one.

HARRY: It's a way of talking.

    (*Pause.*)

BELLA: I didn't mean anything.

HARRY: I know.

    (HARRY *plays with* BELLA's *hair, now falling straight to her shoulders.*)

    You look like a mermaid.

BELLA: A mermaid who can't swim.

HARRY: I'll teach you . . .

BELLA (*laughing, but with an edge*): No thanks . . . I've had my dip for today.

    (*Pause.*)

    Do you usually have sex?

HARRY (*mock shock*): I beg your pardon.

BELLA: When you come out here . . .?

HARRY: It all depends.

BELLA: On the girls?

HARRY: It depends how it works out.

BELLA: How do you mean?

HARRY: Well . . . one day we came here with a couple of girls. We had a great time. But there was nothing. On the way back we stopped at a pub . . . I'll never forget this bloke singing 'The Wayward Wind' . . . he was absolutely legless . . . and whenever any of us looked at each other we were all in fits laughing. It was a great night . . . and there was nothing. On the way back we stopped the car and climbed over a fence into a field——

BELLA: Oh aye?

HARRY: —no, we were all dying for, you know, and the girls went off down the field in the dark, and when they came back somebody said 'Look at the sky!' because it was all crammed with stars . . . and we all stood there for a minute like a gang of kids, staring at the stars . . . and then . . . we climbed back over the fence and got in the car and drove back and dropped the girls at their place and . . . that was all. . . . There was nothing.

BELLA: Didn't you fancy them?

HARRY: Don't you believe me?

BELLA: Yeah but——

HARRY: —it sounds funny?

BELLA: Yeah.

HARRY (*wry*): It sounds funny to me too.
    (*Pause.*)

BELLA: Did you fancy us?

HARRY: Yeah.

BELLA: Did you?

HARRY (*laughing*): You knew that!

BELLA: Yeah . . .

HARRY: You know that . . . don't you . . .
    (*Pause.* BELLA *idly traces in the sand.*)

BELLA: You courting?

HARRY: Courting?

BELLA: Yeah . . . going steady . . .

HARRY: On and off.
    (*Pause.*)
    You know . . . it's nothing serious, purely sexual.

BELLA: Is it?

HARRY: Always is.

BELLA: How about your mate?

HARRY: He's crazy about the Reds, wouldn't miss a game.

(*Pause.*)

BELLA: Did you go to that club?

HARRY: Which?

BELLA: The one he was talking about . . . the one where he was painting . . .

HARRY: I went in there . . . couple of times.

BELLA: Did you like it?

HARRY: I didn't rave about it.

BELLA: I used to go there.

HARRY: Did you?

BELLA: Yeah . . .

HARRY: With your mate?

BELLA: No . . . a few years back . . . before I met her.

HARRY: You go with a gang?

BELLA (*smiling*): Yeah . . . there was a big gang of us. (*Laughing.*) We were all crazy.

HARRY: How old?

BELLA: Eh?

HARRY: How old was the gang?

BELLA: Oh, we were all still at school . . . we had a terrific time. You know . . . we didn't care about anything . . .

HARRY: Yeah.

BELLA: Seems ages and ages ago.

HARRY: How old are you now?

(BELLA *traces in the sand.*)

BELLA: There.

HARRY: What?

BELLA: There . . . see?

HARRY (*scrutinizing*): Sixty-nine?

BELLA: That's what I feel!

HARRY: I can't read it . . .

BELLA (*spelling out*): Over . . . the . . . hill . . .

HARRY: You . . . over the hill?

BELLA: Yeah.

(*Pause.*)

(HARRY *looks at* BELLA, *curiously.*)

HARRY: How old are you?

BELLA: Guess.

HARRY: No . . . I want to know.

BELLA: Why?

HARRY: Nosey.

BELLA (*laughs*): No secret. Nineteen.

HARRY: Nineteen?

BELLA: Yeah.

HARRY: And over the hill?

BELLA: Yeah . . .

    (*Pause.*)

HARRY (*hot gospelling*): But look here, young lady! Don't yuh know the whole of life lies ahead of yuh? Think of all the wonderful things life has to offer yuh! Be grateful for the wonderful gifts . . .

BELLA: The night I was seventeen I cried my eyes out.

HARRY (*mildly*): Did you? (*Pause.*) Why?

    (BELLA *shrugs.*)

BELLA: Your mate was right about that club.

HARRY: What? The Ladies?

BELLA: Yeah . . .

HARRY: Would you feel any better if I told you about the Gents?

BELLA (*laughs*): No thanks! (*Pause.*) Were they just as bad?

HARRY: Worse. (*Pause.*) It's getting cooler isn't it?

BELLA: It's nice.

HARRY: Yeah . . .

    (*Pause.* HARRY *looks towards the woods.*)

    They're taking their time . . .

BELLA (*shy giggle*): Well . . .

HARRY (*prissy*): Not that *I* care.

BELLA: There you go . . .

    (*Pause. They look at each other, look away.* BELLA *sighs.*)

    Work tomorrow.

HARRY (*mock-indignant*): Don't you like your work?

BELLA (*wry*): Oh yeah!

HARRY: Well . . . I mean . . . you'll never make a professional footballer.

BELLA (*laughs*): Noooo . . .

    (*Pause.* HARRY *takes out the cigarettes.*)

HARRY: Wanna smoke?

BELLA: Me throat's too dry.
HARRY: We'll get a drink soon.
　　(HARRY *takes out a cigarette.*)
BELLA: Here y'are.
　　(*She lights it for him. Silence.* TIM *returns, sits.*)
　　Where's Marie?
TIM (*smiles*): Chasing squirrels.
BELLA (*amazed*): Squirrels?
TIM: Yeah. (*Then to* HARRY.) Give us a drag.
　　(HARRY *passes the cigarette.* TIM *puffs it and gives it back.*)
　　Ta. I was dying for that.
　　(*Pause.* TIM *looks at the other two.*)
　　(MARIE *returns. Stands.*)
MARIE (*excited*): Hey, Bella . . . guess what we saw in the woods!
BELLA: A squirrel.
MARIE (*disappointed*): Oh. (*Then to* TIM.) You told them.
BELLA: What was it like?
MARIE (*eager*): It was red. A red squirrel . . . in the woods.
HARRY (*grins*): Have you never seen a squirrel before?
MARIE (*straight*): No.
BELLA: Neither have I.
TIM: It came right up to us.
MARIE: Yeah! It wasn't frightened or anything.
HARRY: You can feed them.
MARIE (*thrilled*): Feed them? Can you?
HARRY: Yeah . . . there's a Squirrel Reserve . . . further up the
　　beach . . . and the squirrels come right up to the wire
　　netting and stick their heads through for food.
MARIE: Go way!
HARRY: They do. Don't they, Tim?
TIM: Yeah. They're not shy. You can feed them.
MARIE: Isn't that great!
BELLA: I'd love to do that.
MARIE: Yeah . . . I would too.
BELLA: Could we do that?
HARRY: What are we gonna feed them?
MARIE (*wry*): Oh aye.
　　(*They chuckle.*)

E　　　　　　　　　　65

BELLA: I'd love that, though. I'd love to feed them.

TIM: Do it another time.

MARIE: What do you feed them?

HARRY: Smoky bacon crisps.

MARIE: You what?

HARRY: Smoky bacon crisps.

MARIE (*laughs*): Crisp off!

HARRY (*injured*): You do.

MARIE (*hooting*): Smoky bacon crisps!

HARRY: They'll touch nothing else.

MARIE: I thought they ate nuts?

HARRY: Noooo . . . smoky bacon crisps or nothing. That's their diet. (*Pause.*) If you catch one young it makes a very tasty dinner.

MARIE: Oh . . . sod off!

HARRY: Smoky bacon squirrel . . . delicious.

MARIE: Ughhh.

(*The foursome sit in a circle. Pause.*)

(*To* BELLA.) You haven't half caught the sun!

BELLA: Yeah . . . I'm burning.

MARIE: Have I?

BELLA: You're all red.

MARIE: Great! (*Sly grin.*) I'm sore too . . .

BELLA (*chuckles*): Oohhh . . . was he rough?

MARIE: Wild.

TIM: I was driven to it.

(*Silence.* BELLA *goes to the top of the dune, looks across the river. She hitches the towel across her shoulders and comes down.*)

MARIE: You look like the Queen of the May.

BELLA (*smiles*): I *was* the Queen of the May!

MARIE: Oh aye?

BELLA: Two years running. I was made up with meself. Two years running I was picked to lead the procession down our street. I had long blonde hair . . . real blonde . . . and I had me ma's dress on, and me sister's shoes, and lace curtains for a veil, and I went clumping along at the head of the procession, two years running. I thought I was lovely.

66

(*Pause. Laughs, wry.*) Then I got me National Health specs
and nobody wanted to know. Huh . . . I wouldn't go out in
them, anyway. (*Pause.*) Still . . . I was the Queen of the
May . . . two years running . . . I've got a photograph of it
. . . I looked lovely . . . with me long blonde hair . . .
looked a little angel!
 (*Silence.*)

HARRY (*to* TIM): Were you ever the Queen of the May?

TIM: I was invited. They were very keen.

HARRY: Too shy, were you?

TIM: I never liked processions.
 (*Pause.*)
 (MARIE *roots in the bag.*)

MARIE: I'm starving.
 (HARRY *picks up a half-eaten sandwich, offers it.*)

HARRY: Here y'are.
 (MARIE *takes it, examines it delicately, bites it.*)

MARIE (*crunching*): It's all fulla sand.
 (MARIE *slings it aside. Silence. She looks at* HARRY.)
 (*Sly grin*): Was your mam up early this morning?

HARRY: Me mam?

MARIE: Yeah.

HARRY: What about me mam?

MARIE: Was she up early this morning?

HARRY: Me mam's always up early.

MARIE: She musta been up early this morning.

HARRY: Eh?
 (*Pause.* MARIE *looks at* BELLA.)

MARIE (*grins*): Who made the butties?

HARRY: You what?

MARIE: Who made the butties?
 (*Silence.* HARRY *glances at* TIM.)
 Who made the butties then?

HARRY: Me.

MARIE: Very nice.

HARRY (*ultra polite*): I'm glad you liked them.

MARIE: Oh, they were very nice.
 (HARRY *stares at her.* MARY *grins back, glances at* BELLA,

67

giggles. HARRY *looks, glances at* TIM, *lies back. Silence.*)

HARRY (*sits up*): I'm so glad you approve.

(HARRY *lies back.* MARIE *giggles. She looks around, licks her lips.*)

MARIE: I'm dying of thirst.

BELLA: Hey . . . wanna tomato?

MARIE: What?

(BELLA *offers the tomato.*)

BELLA: D'you want it?

MARIE: I'll wait for a drink.

TIM: Pubs'll be open soon.

BELLA (*to* TIM): D'you want it?

HARRY (*noble*): We saved that for you.

TIM: Gee . . . shucks!

(TIM *bites the tomato, passes it to* BELLA.)

BELLA: Ta . . .

(BELLA *sucks the tomato, tosses the remains into the sand—* PLOP! *Silence. The men lie back.*)

MARIE (*pokes* HARRY): Where did you get the gloves?

HARRY: You what?

MARIE: Where did you get the gloves?

HARRY: What gloves?

MARIE: The gloves in the van.

HARRY: In the van?

MARIE: I seen a pair of gloves in the van.

HARRY: Did you?

MARIE (*arch*): *Ladies*' gloves.

HARRY: What sharp eyes we have!

MARIE: They were in the glove compartment.

HARRY: I keep all my gloves there.

MARIE: Oh aye?

HARRY: Yeah.

MARIE: Whose is they?

HARRY: Me mam's.

MARIE (*sarcastic*): Oh aye!

HARRY: I gave her a lift to the Post Office.

MARIE: Did you?

HARRY: She won't go out without her gloves on.

MARIE: Won't she?

HARRY: She leaves gloves all over the place.

MARIE: Does she?

HARRY: I'm forever clearing up after her.

(Pause.)

BELLA *(to HARRY, smiling)*: Are you courting?

TIM *(flicks his wrist)*: No, we're just good friends.

(BELLA laughs. HARRY lies back. Silence. MARIE looks up.)

MARIE: Got any ciggies?

HARRY: One.

(HARRY passes the cigarette, gives her a light.)

MARIE *(to BELLA)*: Wanna drag?

BELLA: Ta.

(BELLA puffs, offers it to HARRY.)

D'you wanna drag?

HARRY: Ta.

(HARRY puffs, offers it to TIM.)

TIM: Ta.

(TIM puffs, offers it back to MARIE.)

MARIE: I'm too dry.

BELLA: Yeah . . . I'm parched.

HARRY: They'll soon be open.

TIM: What time is it?

(HARRY gets up and elaborately studies the sun.)

HARRY: Twenty-eight—no! twenty-nine minutes past six. *(Sits.)*
I could just go a pint of bitter. *(Pause.)*

TIM *(licking his lips)*: Yeah . . .

*(Silence. HARRY snaps on the radio, takes BELLA's hand,
stands.)*

HARRY: Let's have a dance.

BELLA *(delighted)*: Yeah.

(They dance.)

TIM *(ultra polite, to MARIE)*: May I have this dance, please?

MARIE *(disdainful)*: Yeah . . . all right . . .

(They dance.)

*(After a moment, quite naturally, HARRY is facing MARIE and
dancing with her. After this the couples dissolve and the
foursome dance together. Then HARRY faces MARIE again and*

69

begins to clown.)

HARRY: Come on . . .

MARIE (*laughing*): Jesus!

HARRY (*mock indignant*): Come on . . . you're not doing it properly.

MARIE: Where did you learn to dance?

HARRY: All my steps are my own, darling.

(MARIE *tries to copy him, but falls back laughing.* TIM *taps him on the shoulder*.)

TIM: May I cut in?

HARRY (*queer tone*): Certainly.

(*The men dance—ballroom style. The girls look at them, laughing. Then the girls dance, half-heartedly*.)

TIM: Have you been unfaithful again?

HARRY (*hanging his head*): Yes.

TIM: Swine.

HARRY: Sorry . . . (*Pause*.) Have you?

TIM: Yes.

HARRY: With them?

TIM: Yeah . . .

HARRY: Swine.

MARIE: Cheeky buggers!

(MARIE *snaps off the transistor. The four sit down*.)

(*To* HARRY—*sly grin*): You know last night . . .

HARRY: What?

MARIE: What made you pick us?

HARRY: Pick you?

MARIE: Yeah . . . why did you pick us?

(*Pause.* HARRY *grins*.)

HARRY: You were sitting next to us.

MARIE: Oh, thanks very much!

HARRY: Pleasure.

MARIE: You came and sat next to us. You were sitting somewhere else when we came in. I saw you.

HARRY: Oh aye . . . piping?

MARIE: Huh!

HARRY: No . . . what it was . . . I fancied the barmaid, see.

MARIE: Oh aye? The Chinese girl?

70

HARRY: She's only part time.

MARIE: Oh?

HARRY: Well, I was chatting her up, like, and——

MARIE: She didn't fancy *you*?

HARRY: She was crazy about me. She kept sending me drinks over.

MARIE: What went wrong?

TIM: She didn't have a mate.

HARRY: So we looked around . . . and we decided you'd do . . .

MARIE (*giggling*): Cheeky sod!
    (*Silence.*)

BELLA (*to* HARRY): Hey . . . can we go to that pub . . .

HARRY: What pub?

BELLA: You know . . . the one you were talking about . . . where you went that time before . . . the one where they had the sing song . . .

HARRY (*looks at* TIM): Could do . . .

BELLA: I'd love to go somewhere like that. A singing pub.

MARIE: Yeah . . .

TIM: It's a bit out of the way, that one . . .

BELLA: In the country . . . ?

TIM: Yeah . . .

BELLA: It sounds nice . . .

HARRY: Fancy going back to Liverpool?

TIM: Plenty of pubs there.

MARIE: I'm fed up drinking in town.

BELLA: Let's go to a country pub . . . eh?
    (*Pause.*)

TIM: We'll have a look on the way back.
    (HARRY *stands, puts on his sweater, climbs the dune and looks across the river.*)

HARRY: Hey . . . look at this!

BELLA (*joining him*): What is it?

HARRY: A liner . . . on its way to South America.

BELLA (*laughing*): How do you know it's going to South America?

HARRY (*pompous*): *All* liners go to South America!

BELLA: Wish we were on it.

HARRY (*stares at her*): Have you ever thought of joining the Fire

Service?

BELLA: Oh sure!

(*Pause. They watch the liner.*)

HARRY: When I was a kid I used to lie awake and listen to the foghorns from the river . . . the sounds of the ships . . . the liners going . . . (*deep-voiced*) BEEEEMMMMMM and the little tugs piping . . . (*shrill*) YIPYIPYIP . . and the others going . . . WHOOWHOOWHOO.

BELLA: I'd be a little tug! YIPYIPYIP.

HARRY: BEEEMMMMM.

BELLA: WHOOWHOOWHOO.

HARRY: BEEEEMMMMMM.

BELLA: YIPYIPYIP.

HARRY: BEEEMMMMM.

(TIM *comes behind them.*)

TIM: WHOOWHOOWHOO.

BELLA: YIPYIPYIP.

MARIE: YIPYIPYIP.

(MARIE *stands and joins them. They clown around.*)

HARRY: BEEEEMMMMMMMM.

TIM: WHOOWHOOWHOO.

MARIE: YIPYIPYIP.

BELLA: YIPYIPYIP.

TIM: BEEEEMMMMMMM.

(HARRY *suddenly comes down and sits sulking.*)

HARRY: Not playing any more.

TIM (*joins him*): What's the matter?

HARRY (*petulant*): Not talking.

TIM (*grins*): Oh . . . I'm sorry.

HARRY (*outburst*): *I* was the liner.

TIM: Were you?

HARRY: You *would* have to be a liner as well.

TIM (*laughing*): I'll be a canoe if you like . . .

HARRY: Not speaking.

(*Pause.*)

BELLA (*wry*): Work tomorrow.

MARIE: Yeah . . .

(*Pause.*)

BELLA: Let's have a great night out.

MARIE (*eager*): Yeah.

BELLA: Yeah.

TIM: What time is it?

HARRY: Nearly seven.

TIM: Jesus! We'll soon be in drinking time.

MARIE: Well come 'ead then!

BELLA: Yeah.

> (*They start to dress.*)
>
> (TIM *is putting on his shoes when he stops and stares. Takes something out.*)

TIM: Hey!

MARIE: What?

TIM: Look at this!

BELLA: The lashes! Great!

HARRY: And I searched the bloody sandhill.

BELLA: Great! Now I can go out in style!

> (MARIE *helps* BELLA *put the lashes on. The men sit waiting and watching.*)
>
> How's that?

HARRY: Let's see you blink.

> (BELLA *blinks and puts on a vamp expression.*)
>
> I'll have to get a pair of those meself!
>
> (*The girls make up.*)
>
> (*This is a long session, uninterrupted except for the occasional giggle from the girls, with the men sitting watching motionless, and the transistor playing. The session is prolonged to the point of acute impatience.*)
>
> (*Each girl applies face cream . . . eye shadow . . . eye liner . . . mascara . . . eyebrow pencil . . . lipstick . . .*)

MARIE (*to* TIM): Wanna try some? (*Laughing.*)

TIM (*mock vanity*): Oh . . . I rely on my bone structure.

> (. . . *When the facial treatment is completed,* MARIE *holds up the mirror while* BELLA *back-combs her hair and then sprays it with lacquer;* BELLA *then holds the mirror while* MARIE *does her hair. Each girl then applies perfume to her neck, ears, chest and wrists. As appropriate, the girls apply the perfume to each other.*)

(*The girls collect their things together.*)

MARIE: You right?

BELLA: Yeah . . .

MARIE: Before we go . . . (*Nods towards the woods.*)

BELLA: Oh yeah . . .

MARIE (*to* TIM): Just a quick one. (*Laughs.*)

(*The men begin to collect the orange peel, papers etc., and put them in a newspaper. They stop and look at each other.* TIM *holds up a towel.*)

TIM: Smell that.

HARRY (*rolling his eyes*): Phew . . .

TIM: There's orange peel all over the place . . .

(TIM *throws down some peelings. The two men look at each other and grin.*)

HARRY: You're thinking what I'm thinking.

(BELLA *comes on, followed by* MARIE. MARIE *stops at the top of the dune. She holds her skirt high and rubs her leg.*)

MARIE (*laughing*): Sorry, lads . . . it's the drips!

(*The men stare.*)

You right?

TIM: Yeah . . . go on . . . we'll just finish getting the things.

(*The girls go off right.*)

(*The men stand still, looking at each other for a minute.* TIM *grins.* HARRY *closes his eyes and laughs quietly.*)

HARRY: It's the drips!

TIM: We better hurry up.

(*They finish collecting their things hastily.*)

HARRY: If we cut through the woods we'll get to the van well before them.

TIM: We don't wanna take any chances.

HARRY: No . . .

TIM: We better move.

HARRY: Yeah . . . they'll get a lift.

TIM (*laughs*): They'll get a lift!

HARRY: Let's get out.

TIM: We'll just make it for Benediction!

HARRY: I'm dying for a pint . . .

TIM: Where'll we go?

HARRY: The opposite way from here.

(TIM *kicks sand over the pile of peelings, etc.*)

TIM: Go quiet while we're in the wood . . .

HARRY: . . . then we can run . . .

TIM: . . . run like buggery!

(HARRY *picks up the transistor and turns it off. They exit left to the woods.*)

HARRY (*laughing*): Dirty cows!

TIM (*laughing*): Dirty cows!

CURTAIN